THE BEST JOKE BOOK #2 BOOK for kids

...with great ghoulie and monster riddles

compiled, collected, and
laughed over by the kids of
JOAN ECKSTEIN and **JOYCE GLEIT**
illustrations by
JOE KOHL

AN AVON CAMELOT BOOK

THE BEST JOKE BOOK FOR KIDS #2 is an original publication of
Avon Books. This work has never before appeared in book form.

AVON BOOKS
A division of
The Hearst Corporation
1790 Broadway
New York, New York 10019

Library of Congress Cataloging in Publication Data:
Eckstein, Joan.
    The best joke book for kids #2.
    (An Avon Camelot book)
    Summary: A collection of jokes and riddles, including knock-knocks, tongue
twisters, and one-liners.
    1. American wit and humor. 2. Wit and humor, Juvenile. [1. Jokes.
2. Riddles] I. Gleit, Joyce. II. Kohl, Joe, ill. III. Title.
PN6163.E25   1987   818'.5402   86-25906

First Camelot Printing: March 1987

CAMELOT TRADEMARK REG. U.S. PAT. OFF AND IN OTHER COUNTRIES, MARCA
REGISTRADA, HECHO EN U.S.A.

Printed in the U.S.A.

OPM 10 9 8 7 6 5 4 3 2 1

Dedicated once again to the kids who made it all possible:
Paul, Jonathan, Lisa, and Stefanie, and all of you.

Terrible Tickles

MAX: I hate school! The teachers hate me, the kids call me four-eyes, nobody talks to me. I'm not going back.
MA: You have to go back.
MAX: Why?
MA: Because you're the principal.

Once upon a time Old King Cole issued an order to his cooks. "From now on," he decreed, "chopped cabbage must be mixed with mayonnaise." To this day his decree is known as Cole's Law.

Two Boy Scouts from the city were on a camping trip. The mosquitoes were so fierce the boys had to hide under their blankets to keep from being bitten. Then one of them saw some lightning bugs, and he said to his friend, "We might as well give up. They're coming after us with flashlights."

Big Al is a nasty, insulting man who owns a grocery store. One day a man came into his store carrying a chicken under his arm. Big Al said to him, "What are you doing with that pig?" The man replied, "You jerk, can't you see this is a chicken, not a pig?" Big Al answered, "I wasn't talking to you, I was talking to the chicken."

A city boy went to the country for his vacation. His first day on the farm he watched the farmer's wife pluck a chicken. Finally he asked, "Do you have to take their clothes off every night?"

BO: Every morning my dog and I go for a tramp in the woods.
BUB: Does your dog enjoy it?
BO: Yes, he loves it, but the tramp is getting a little fed up.

An irate customer goes into a repair shop and says to the salesman, "Look at these shoes you returned to me. One is black and the other's brown!" The shoemaker says, looking puzzled, "Isn't that something? That's the second time that's happened today."

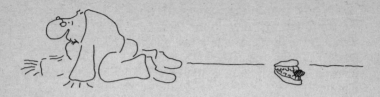

The movie was at a dramatic moment when a woman was disturbed by an old man looking for something on the floor. "What did you lose?" the woman asked in an irritated voice. "A caramel," the old man replied. "A caramel?" she said. "Do you mean to say that you're disturbing me and everyone else for a caramel?" "Yes," said the old man, continuing to look. "My teeth are in it."

A lady brought her beat-up car to the car wash. "Can you make my car look better?" she asked. "Sorry, lady," replied the attendant, "we only wash cars here, we don't iron them."

A man went to his doctor complaining about terrible neck pains, throbbing headaches, and dizzy spells. The doctor examined him and said, "I'm afraid I have some bad news for you. You only have six months to live." The doomed man decided he would spend his remaining time on earth enjoying himself. He told his boss what he thought of him and quit his job. Then he took all his money out of the bank and bought a sports car, ten new suits, and twenty-five pairs of shoes. Then he went to the best shop in town to get himself a dozen tailored shirts. The tailor measured him and wrote down size sixteen neck. "Wait a minute," the man said, "I always wear a size fourteen neck, and that's what I want." "I'll be glad to do it for you, sir," the tailor said. "However, if you wear a size fourteen neck you're going to get terrible neck pains, throbbing headaches, and dizzy spells."

JOHN: I'm sorry, but I can't lend you a dollar.
SAM: You're cheap.
JOHN: No, I'm not. I just don't believe in passing the buck.

JANE: I hope you like the dictionary I bought you for Christmas.
ANNE: Yes, I just can't find the words to thank you.

FIRST HUNTER: I shot one bullet and two rabbits died.
SECOND HUNTER: That's nothing. I shot one bullet and five hundred frogs croaked.

Three men were sitting on a park
bench. The man in the middle was
reading a newspaper. The two men on
either side were going through the
motions as if they were actually fishing.
They carefully baited their hooks, cast
out their lines, and then reeled them in
when they had an imaginary bite. A
policeman stopped when he saw what
was going on. Puzzled, he asked the
man in the middle if he knew the two
men on either side. The man folded his
newspaper and admitted they were his
friends. "In that case," the policeman
warned, "you'd better get them out of
here." "Yes, Officer," the man replied,
and then he began to row furiously.

LAWYER READING THE WILL OF A
MISERLY MILLIONAIRE:"... and to my
dear nephew John, whom I promised
to remember in my will, 'Hi there,
John.'"

Once there was an evil man named Peter Prankster, who had an evil eye. He could take one look at you and zap you. Everyone was afraid of Pete's Zap Eye.

BO: My pet died and I can't understand it. He was the picture of health.
BUB: You must have been looking at the negative.

BO: Boy, am I mad! The telephone company had the nerve to send me a bill.
BUB: Did you pay it?
BO: Of course not. I believe in free speech.

DAD: What are you learning in math, Suzie?
SUZIE: Gozinta, Daddy.
DAD: Is that a new computer language?
SUZIE: No, it's just gozinta. Like, two gozinta four twice, four gozinta twelve three times.

BO: I have music in my very soul.
BUB: You're right. I did hear your shoes squeak.

A lady bought a stamp at the post office and asked the clerk, "Shall I stick it on myself?" The clerk replied, "It'll get there a lot faster if you stick it on the envelope."

A little boy came home from his first day at school. He said, "I'm not going back tomorrow." His mother asked, "Why not?" and he said, "Well, I can't read, I can't write, and they won't let me talk, so what's the use?"

BO: How do you like your new teacher?
BUB: I don't. She told me to sit up front for the present, and then she didn't give me the present.

Father took his kid to the opera. The conductor waved his baton and the soprano sang. The kid wanted to know why was he hitting her. "He isn't hitting her," the father replied. "Then why is the lady screaming?" asked the boy.

MOTHER: Ever since my son was a little boy he always wanted to be a magician and saw people in half.
FRIEND: Is he your only child?
MOTHER: No, he has several half brothers and sisters.

AGENT TO WRITER: I've got some good news and some bad news.
WRITER: First tell me the good news.
AGENT: Paramount just loved your story, absolutely ate it up.
WRITER: That's fantastic! And the bad news?
AGENT: Paramount is my dog.

MOTHER: If you don't turn off that loud music right now, I'll go insane.
SON: Too late, I turned it off an hour ago.

BO: Does your dog have a license?
BUB: No. He's not old enough to drive yet.

Tough luck, said the egg in the monastery... out of the frying pan into the friar.

FIRST WOMAN: I went to the theater last night, but I had to leave after Act One.
SECOND WOMAN: Why was that?
FIRST WOMAN: Well, the program said, Act Two, one month later, and I couldn't wait.

PATIENT TO DOCTOR: A miraculous recovery? Thank God. I was afraid I would have to pay you.

Did you hear about the scientist who crossed a chicken with a silkworm and got a hen that lays eggs with panty hose on them?

FIRST RANCHER: What's the name of your place?
SECOND RANCHER: The SYF Lazy R Double Snake Square Q Bar Z.
FIRST RANCHER: How many head of cattle do you have?
SECOND RANCHER: Only a few. Not many survive the branding.

JUDGE: I see that in addition to stealing money, you took watches, rings, and pearls.
CROOK: Yes, Your Honor. I was taught that money alone doesn't bring happiness.

Some scuba-diving students were about to be tested on their first dive in the ocean. "What do we have to do to pass?" asked one. The instructor replied, "Come back."

EMPLOYEE: Could I have a raise?
BOSS: Impossible. You've only been here two weeks. You have to work yourself up first.
EMPLOYEE: I already have. Look, I'm trembling all over.

Did you hear about the boy who stayed up all night wondering where the sun went? It finally dawned on him.

BEGGAR: Can you give me thirty cents?
MAN: I only have a quarter.
BEGGAR: So now you owe me five cents.

A man in an old wreck of a truck drew up to a tollbooth. "Seventy-five cents," said the toll collector. "Sold!" said the driver.

BO: What do you do when a health-food salesman knocks at your door?
BUB: Go ahead and vitamin.

Two Martians landed on a corner right in front of a traffic light. "I saw her first," one Martian said. "So what?" replied the other. "I'm the one she winked at."

BANK ROBBER *(in a low voice):* Put the money in a bag, sucker, and don't move.
TELLER *(in a whisper):* Straighten your tie, sucker. They're taking your picture.

Favorite Knock-Knocks

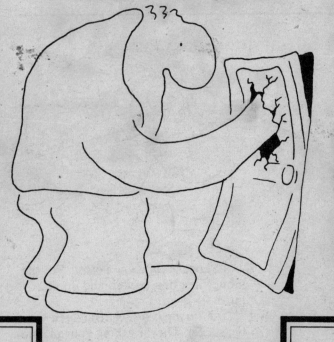

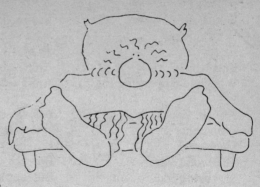

Knock, knock.
Who's there?
Fiddlestick.
Fiddlestick who?
If the bed's too short your fiddle stick out.

Knock, knock.
Who's there?
Alfred.
Alfred who?
Alfred the needle if you sew the button on.

Knock, knock.
Who's there?
Little old lady.
Little old lady who?
I didn't know you could yodel.

Knock, knock.
Who's there?
Arthur.
Arthur who?
Arthur any more hamburgers?

Knock, knock.
Who's there?
Boo.
Boo who?
What are you crying for?

Knock, knock.
Who's there?
Sherwood.
Sherwood who?
Sherwood like to come in.

Knock, knock.
Who's there?
Anita.
Anita who?
Anita a bite to eat.

Knock, knock.
Who's there?
Butcher.
Butcher who?
Butcher arms around me.

Knock, knock.
Who's there?
Orange juice.
Orange juice who?
Orange juice sorry now?

Knock, knock.
Who's there?
Mister.
Mister who?
Mister bus home from school.

Ticklers from Bo and Bub

BO: When I'm down in the dumps I buy
some new clothes.
BUB: So that's where you get them.

BO: I think you need new glasses.
BUB: Why? I just got these.
BO: I knew as soon as you came in the window.

BO: I'm going away to study singing.
BUB: Good. How far away?

BO: Do you know they invented something
that can let you see right through walls?
BUB: Really? What?
BO: They're calling it windows.

BO: Hey, look out the window and see if
the traffic blinker is working.
BUB: Yes. No. Yes. No. Yes. No. Yes. No.

BO: Do you know what keeps the moon
in place?
BUB: What?
BO: Its beams.

BO: I spent two hours over my history books
last night.
BUB: You really studied, didn't you?
BO: Who said anything about studying?
The books were under my bed.

BUB: What's one and one?
BO: Two.
BUB: What's four minus two?
BO: Two.
BUB: Who wrote Tom Sawyer?
BO: Twain.
BUB: Now say all the answers together.
BO: Too Two Twain.
BUB: Have a nice twip.

BO: I can't sleep. What shall I do?
BUB: Lie near the edge of the bed and you'll
drop right off.

BO: There's a man outside with a wooden leg
named Jones.
BUB: What's the name of his other leg?

BO: Where shall we meet?
BUB: Under the clothesline.
BO: Why under the clothesline?
BUB: That's where I hang out.

BO: Our dog is just like one of the family.
BUB: Which one?

BO: Every night, I take two quarters to bed with me.
BUB: Why?
BO: They are my sleeping quarters.

BO: What has four legs and goes "Oom, oom"?
BUB: What?
BO: A cow walking backwards.

BO: My mom wants me to go to the store to buy some toothpaste.
BUB: Why? Are her teeth loose?

BO: How can you make pants last?
BUB: Make the jackets and vests first.

BO: Have you seen me on television?
BUB: On and off.
BO: How'd you like me?
BO: Off.

BO: Why do Norwegians say "skoal" when they drink?
BUB: Because it is—if there's ice in the drink.

BO: I once spent many months with an
Indian tribe, learning their dances.
Afterwards, they gave me an Indian name.
BUB: What is it?
BO: Clumsy.

BO: Where do you bathe?
BUB: In the spring.
BO: I didn't ask you when, I asked you
where.

BO: Do you realize it takes three sheep to make one sweater?
BUB: I didn't even know they could knit.

BO: Some guy told me I look just like you.
BUB: Oh yeah? What did you say?
BO: Nothing. He was bigger than me.

BO *(holding hands behind back)*: You want to see my new mattababy?
BUB: What's a mattababy?
BO: Nothing, honey—whatsamatter with you?

BO: Last night I put my tooth under my pillow, and this morning I woke up and found a dime.
BUB: That's nothing. I put my tooth under my pillow and got a dollar.
BO: That's because you have buck teeth.

BO: Why did the chef put a giant firecracker under a platter of pancakes?
BUB: He wanted to blow his stack.

BO: Did Adam and Eve ever have a date?
BUB: No. They had an apple.

BO: I just got a bottle of vodka for my mother-in-law.
BUB: Sounds like a good swap.

BUB: Name two pronouns.
BO: Who, me?

Crazy Riddles

How can you fall over forty feet and
not get hurt?
   Move from the front to the rear of a
crowded bus.

What happened when the boarding-
house blew up?
   Roomers were flying.

What gets wetter the more it dries?
   A towel.

Why do people go to nudists' camps?
   To air their differences.

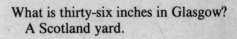

Where do old Volkswagens go?
   To an old Volks home.

What is thirty-six inches in Glasgow?
   A Scotland yard.

What month has twenty-eight days?
   All of them.

Two wrongs never make a right, but
what did two rights make?
   The first airplane.

Why does a small candle hurt when it
is lit?
   It gets glowing pains.

Why did the little girl stand in front of the mirror with her eyes closed?
    So she could see how she looked when she was asleep.

If a man is born in England, grows up in Germany, comes to America, and dies in Philadelphia, what is he?
    Dead.

Why was the boy surprised to find cucumbers growing from his ears?
    He planted carrots.

Why did Robin Hood rob the rich?
    Because the poor didn't have any money.

Why doesn't a bald-headed man need keys?
    He doesn't have any locks.

What did the digital watch say to his mother?
    Look, Mom, no hands.

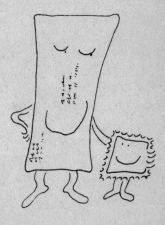

What did the letter say to the stamp?
    Stick with me and we'll go places.

Why is bowling such a quiet sport?
 Because when you play you can hear
a pin drop.

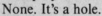
Why couldn't Cinderella play football?
 Because she had a pumpkin for a
coach.

What did Baby Corn say to Mommy
Corn?
 Where's the Pop Corn?

How much dirt is there in a hole three
feet deep by six feet?
 None. It's a hole.

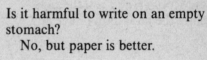

Is it harmful to write on an empty
stomach?
 No, but paper is better.

What can you never have for breakfast?
 Lunch and dinner.

Why does it get hot after a basketball game?
 Because all the fans have gone.

How do you keep milk from turning
sour?
 Keep it in the cow.

What's Up, Doc???

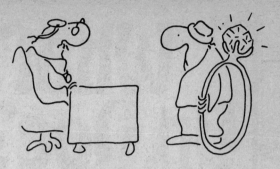

PATIENT: Can a person be in love with an elephant?
DOCTOR: No.
PATIENT: Do you know anyone who wants to buy a very large engagement ring?

BO: What do you call a doctor who treats ducks?
BUB: A quack.

EYE DOCTOR: You need glasses.
PATIENT: I'm already wearing glasses.
EYE DOCTOR: In that case, I need glasses.

DOCTOR: Your cough sounds much better today.
PATIENT: It should. I practiced all night.

PARENT: Junior has just swallowed a bullet. What should I do?
DOCTOR: Don't point him at anybody.

Loose Limericks

There was a young person named Ned,
Who dined before going to bed
On lobster and ham
And pickles and jam,
And when he awoke he was dead.

A daring young salesman of Leeds
Rashly swallowed six packets of seeds.
In a month, silly ass,
He was covered with grass,
And he couldn't sit down for the weeds.

A glamorous dame named McFall
Wore a newspaper gown to the ball.
The costume caught fire
And burned up her entire
Front page, sports pages, and all.

There was a young person named Bright,
Whose speed was much faster than light.
She set out one day
In a relative way
And returned on the previous night.

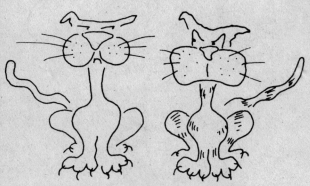

There once were two cats of Kilkenny.
Each thought there was one cat too many.
So they scratched and they fit,
And they tore and they bit,
Till instead of two cats there weren't any.

Tasty Ticklers

What kind of fish goes with peanut butter?
   Jellyfish.

What do you get when you cross a cabbage and a tiger?
   Man-eating coleslaw.

BEGGAR: Pardon me, but would you give me fifty cents for a sandwich?
PASSERBY: I don't know. Let me see the sandwich.

CUSTOMER: How do you serve shrimps here?
WAITER: We bend down.

CUSTOMER: Why is this doughnut all smashed up?
WAITER: You said you wanted a cup of coffee and a doughnut and to step on it, so I did.

CUSTOMER: Have you any wild duck?
WAITER: No, madame, but we can take a tame one and irritate him for you.

BO: Do you feel like a cup of coffee?
BUB: Of course not. Why, do I look like one?

CUSTOMER: Waiter, what kind of soup is this? It tastes like soap. I ordered pea soup.
WAITER: Oh, sorry, my mistake. That's tomato soup. The pea soup tastes like mud.

BO: Can you eat fried chicken with your fingers?
BUB: No, fingers should be eaten separately.

WAITER: Would you like your coffee black?

CUSTOMER: I don't know. What other colors do you have?

BO: What's the worst thing you can find in our school cafeteria?

BUB: The food.

CUSTOMER: Waiter, this soup isn't fit for a pig.

WAITER: I'll take it back, sir, and bring some that is.

CUSTOMER: I can't eat this soup.

WAITER: I'll get the manager.

CUSTOMER: I can't eat this soup.

MANAGER: I'll get the chef.

CUSTOMER: I can't eat this soup.

CHEF: What's wrong with the soup?

CUSTOMER: Nothing. I don't have a spoon.

BO: How do you like the pound cake I made?
BUB: You didn't pound it enough.

BO: What's the word for midgets in cannibal language?
BUB: I don't know.
BO: Snacks.

Why did the coffee taste like mud?
Because it was ground only five minutes ago.

BO: What kind of bird tastes like fish?
BUB: I don't know.
BO: Hadduck.

Terrific Tongue Twisters

A flea and a fly in a flue,
Imprisoned, said, "What can we do?"
"Let us flee," said the fly.
"Let us fly," said the flea.
So they flew through a flaw in the flue.

Swan swam over the sea:
Swim, swan, swim.
Swan swam back again:
Well swum, swan.

Three gray geese in the green grass grazing.

His shirt soon shrank in the suds.

The Lethe police dismisseth us.

Say this fast three times: Toy boat.

I go by a Blue Goose bus.

Four fat fryers foolishly fishing for flowers.

43

Frivolous fat Fanny fried fresh fish.

Cross crossings cautiously.

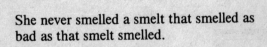

Betty Botter bought some butter.
"But," said she, "this butter's bitter.
If I put it in my batter,
It will make my batter bitter."
So she bought some better butter,
Better than the bitter butter,
And she put the better butter in the bitter batter
And made the bitter batter better.

She never smelled a smelt that smelled as
bad as that smelt smelled.

Goofy Critters

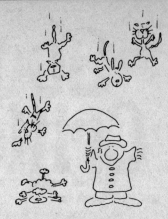

How do you know when it's raining cats and dogs?
   You step into a poodle.

BO: What holiday does a mouse like best?
BUB: Christmouse.

What's the difference between a cat and a frog?
   A cat has nine lives, but a frog croaks all the time.

Why does a baby pig eat so much?
   To make a hog of himself.

What happens when you give lemons to your cat?
  You get a sour puss.

Why are elephants gray?
  So you can tell them apart from the blueberries.

How do you get down from an elephant?
  You don't get down from an elephant, you get down from a goose.

How do you make a slow horse fast?
  Don't give him anything to eat.

BO: What will you get if you cross a dog and a cat?
BUB: An animal that chases itself.

BO: What do you put on a bad pig?
BUB: Hamcuffs.

Why did the moth eat the rug?
    Because he wanted to see the floor show.

What did the chicken say when it laid a square egg?
    Ouch!

Why do birds fly south?
    Because it's too far to walk.

Why can't two elephants go swimming at
the same time?
Because they only have one pair of trunks.

BO: Is a chicken big enough to eat when it's
two weeks old?
BUB: No, of course not!
BO: Then how does it keep from starving?

Why was the mommy flea sad?
Because her children were going to the
dogs.

What is a fast duck?
A quick quack.

BO: I wish I had the money to buy an
elephant.
BUB: What do you want with an elephant?
BO: Nothing, I just want the money.

What did the leopard say when he finished
his lunch?
Hmm, that hit the spot, the spot, the
spot...

What is black and white and red all over?
 An embarrassed zebra.

BO: Why was the crow sitting on the
telephone wire?
BUB: Why?
BO: He wanted to make a long-distance caw.

BO: What do you call a squirrel's nest?
BUB: A nutcracker's suite.

BO: What kind of mothers let their children
gain twenty pounds a week?
BUB: Elephant mothers.

BO: Have you ever seen a fish cry?
BUB: No, but I've seen a whale blubber.

BO: Have you ever hunted bear?
BUB: No, but I have gone fishing in my
shorts.

One day, a woman saw a man holding a frog in his hands. She asked him, "Where are you going with that frog?" "I'm taking him to the zoo," the man answered. The next day, she saw the same man, still holding the frog. "I thought you took the frog to the zoo," she said. "I did take him to the zoo yesterday," the man replied. "Today I'm taking him to the movies."

BO: Why does a polar bear wear a fur coat?
BUB: Because he'd look funny in a tweed one.

BO: I'd like a pair of alligator shoes.
BUB: Oh, really? What size does your alligator wear?

Why do dogs growl?
   Because they don't know any swear words.

BO: What do you call an arrogant insect?
BUB: A cocky roach.

BO: That's a strange-looking dog.
BUB: He's a genuine police dog.
BO: He doesn't look like any police dog I've ever seen.
BUB: Of course not, he's in the Secret Service.

How do you catch a monkey?

Hang upside down in a tree and make a noise like a banana.

BO: What's the difference between an elephant and an orange?
BUB: I don't know.
BO: I would hate to send you to the store for oranges.

What do elephants have that no other animal has?

Baby elephants.

How do you find a lost dog in the woods?

Put your ear to a tree and listen to the bark.

BO: The big brown bear at the zoo just had a little baby bear, and they want to do a story on it.
BUB: I guess they'll send a cub reporter, huh?

BO: Sis, did you hear what happened at the flea circus?
BUB: No. What happened?
BO: A dog came along and stole the show.

BUB: If you were in the jungle and an elephant charged you, what would you do?
BO: Pay him.

The little boy noticed some green parakeets
in the pet-shop window. "Look, Mom,
there's some canaries that aren't ripe yet."

How do you make an elephant float?
    Take two scoops of ice cream, then add
an elephant and a quart of root beer.

BO: That's a great-looking stuffed lion.
Where did you get him?
BUB: In Africa, when I was on a hunting
expedition with my uncle.
BO: What's he stuffed with?
BUB: My uncle.

BO: My little dog is not feeling well.
BUB: Oh, he must be a pupsickle.

BO: How do you make an elephant fly?
BUB: I'm not sure, but I know you're going
to need a pretty huge zipper.

A duck, a frog, and a skunk went to the fair. Tickets were a dollar. Who got in and who didn't?

The duck got in because it had a bill. The frog got in because it had a green back. But the skunk couldn't get in because it only had a scent and it was bad.

A kangaroo goes into a bar and orders a beer. The bartender puts the beer down in front of the kangaroo and says, "That'll be three dollars." A man sitting next to the kangaroo says, "Pardon me for being nosy, but I've never seen a kangaroo in a bar before." "Yeah," replies the kangaroo, " and at three dollars for a beer you probably won't see many more."

BO: Why do elephants paint their toenails red?
BUB: I don't know. Why?
BO: So they can hide in the strawberry patch.
BUB: I don't believe that.
BO: Did you ever see an elephant in a strawberry patch?
BUB: No.
BO: See, it works.

How do you keep a turkey in suspense?
   I'll tell you tomorrow.

Why do elephants have trunks?
   Because they don't have glove compartments.

What did the beaver say to the tree?
   It's been nice gnawing you.

BO: A snake just snapped at me.
BUB: Don't be silly, snakes don't snap.
BO: This one did—it was a garter snake.

BO: Is it true that an alligator won't attack you if you carry a flashlight?
BUB: That depends on how fast you carry it.

Why did the elephant have holes in his hide?
   He forgot to put mothballs in his trunk.

Winning One-Liners

An igloo is an icicle built for two.

Retired teachers have no principals.

Ministers make parson-to-parson calls.

It takes guts to string a guitar.

Canaries are not expensive, they're cheep.

Hummingbirds hum because they don't know the words.

Cannibals have their friends for lunch.

A pedestrian can be reached by car.

A sword swallower went on a diet and was on pins and needles for three months.

A composer who takes lots of showers probably writes soap operas.

It was Eli Whitney who said, "Keep your cotton-pickin' hands off my gin!"

The doggie who just loves getting washed five times a day is a shampoodle.

My teacher calls me scuba because my grades are below C level.

My brother is so dumb he thinks high school has to be up on a hill.

Ghoulies
and
Monsters

FIRST INVISIBLE MAN: Did you miss me when
I was gone?
SECOND INVISIBLE MAN: Were you gone?

ANNOUNCER OF TV HORROR SHOW: *The
Invisible Man* will not be seen tonight.

ONE SKELETON TO THE OTHER: If we had any
guts we'd get out of here.

What's a monster's normal eyesight?
Twenty-twenty-twenty-twenty.

"Mommy, all the kids say I look like a
werewolf."
"Shut up and comb your face."

How does a monster count to fifty?
  On his fingers.

BO: Where would a werewolf go to replace
his tail?
BUB: He would go to any re-tail store.

What flies at night and goes chomp, chomp,
ouch?
  A vampire with a toothache.

BO: What did the boy monster say to the
girl monster?
BUB: What?
BO: I want to hold your hand, hand, hand,
hand, hand.

BO: What do you do with a green monster?
BUB: What?
BO: You wait till it ripens.

If an undertaker buries a body in the wrong place, is that a grave mistake?

What does a vampire put on at the beach?
  Moontan lotion.

Two Martians who just landed were walking down an empty street. They stopped at a fire hydrant. The first Martian said to the fire hydrant, "Take us to your leader...Hey, didn't you hear what I said? Take us to your leader!" The Martians waited. Silence. The first Martian began to kick the hydrant angrily. "Unless you take us to your—" The second Martian said, "Oh, lay off, can't you see he's only a kid?"

BO: How does a witch tell time?
BUB: How?
BO: With a witch watch.

Two cannibals sat down at a table in a cannibal restaurant. The waiter said, "All we have left is a missionary from Prague. You can each pay for half." "Okay," said the cannibal, "we'll split the Czech."

What does the Martian see in the pan when he's cooking? Unidentified frying objects.